Millie Maker
and the
Clever Concert Plans

Story by Katrina Germein
Illustrations by Isabelle Duffy

Text: Katrina Ge_____
Publishers: Tani_ Mazzeo and E_____
Series consultant: Amanda Sutera
  Hands on Heads Consulting
Editor: Gemma Smith
Project editor: Annabel Smith
Designer: Jess Kelly
Project designer: Danielle Maccarone
Illustrations: Isabelle Duffy
Production controller: Renee Tome

NovaStar

Text © 2024 Cengage Learning Australia Pty Limited
Illustrations © 2024 Cengage Learning Australia Pty Limited

Copyright Notice
This Work is copyright. No part of this Work may be reproduced, stored
in a retrieval system, or transmitted in any form or by any means
without prior written permission of the Publisher. Except as permitted
under the *Copyright Act 1968*, for example any fair dealing for the
purposes of private study, research, criticism or review, subject to
certain limitations. These limitations include: Restricting the copying to a
maximum of one chapter or 10% of this book, whichever is greater;
Providing an appropriate notice and warning with the copies of the
Work disseminated; Taking all reasonable steps to limit access to these
copies to people authorised to receive these copies; Ensuring you hold
the appropriate Licences issued by the Copyright Agency Limited ("CAL"),
supply a remuneration notice to CAL and pay any required fees.

ISBN 978 0 17 033388 7

Cengage Learning Australia
Level 5, 80 Dorcas Street
Southbank VIC 3006 Australia
Phone: 1300 790 853
Email: aust.nelsonprimary@cengage.com

For learning solutions, visit **cengage.com.au**

Printed in China by 1010 Printing International Ltd
1 2 3 4 5 6 7 28 27 26 25 24

*Nelson acknowledges the Traditional Owners and Custodians
of the lands of all First Nations Peoples. We pay respect
to Elders past and present, and extend that respect to
all First Nations Peoples today.*

Contents

Chapter 1

Dancing Disaster

Millie usually liked going to school,
but not today. Today, her class would
start getting ready for the school concert.
Millie didn't want to be in the concert –
not after what had happened last year.

Millie felt her cheeks turn pink just thinking about it. She had crashed into a fake tree during the dance performance, and fallen over on stage. What a disaster! Some people had laughed, and Millie had cried all the way home. She used to love dancing, but not after that.

Millie put on her shoes slowly,
brushed her hair slowly,
and ate her breakfast slowly.

When Dad dropped Millie off at school,
she walked to her classroom slowly.

*There must be a way to skip this year's
concert,* Millie thought. *I just need a
clever plan.*

Chapter 2

Surfing Seagull

Millie felt a little better when she remembered that her class had art in the morning. Her favourite subject!

Millie loved shaping animals from clay and stitching patchwork collages with bits of material. She loved sketching with charcoal and building with boxes.

Millie loved making all kinds of things, which is why Dad had given her the nickname "Millie Maker" in the first place. Most of all, Millie loved drawing and painting.

Millie settled into her favourite seat in the art room, next to her friend Jia. From there, she could see all the paint bottles lined up like a rainbow. If only she could spend the rest of the day making things, instead of worrying about the concert.

After art, Ms Perez told the class that they would be performing the song "Surfing Seagull" for the concert. That's when Millie thought of a clever plan. She put her hand up.

"Ms Perez, could I make the costumes instead of singing and dancing?" she asked.

Ms Perez said that everyone was to make their own costume. Millie frowned.
She didn't want to go on stage *ever again*.

At lunchtime, Millie's friends were talking about the concert. Isali had been given the special part of the surfing seagull, which meant she had a dance solo. Jia was going to be a dolphin, like Millie.

Millie felt relieved that she wasn't the seagull, but she still had to go on stage, and that meant anything could happen. *There must be a way to skip this year's concert*, she thought again.

Chapter 3

A New Plan

Every day after lunch that week, the class practised their performance in the school hall. Isali kept forgetting her dance steps, so Ms Perez asked Millie to help her.

While they practised together, Millie looked around the hall. That's when she had an idea for a new plan.

"Could I make some background things for the concert?" Millie asked Ms Perez. "I want to paint some big waves to hang behind the performers."

"Like a set designer?" asked Jia.

"Yes!" said Millie. "Please can I be a set designer instead of a performer, Ms Perez?"

Ms Perez thought for a moment. Then she agreed. Millie was thrilled. She wouldn't have to perform!

After school, Millie and Dad bought a big roll of paper from the shops.

Millie cheerfully drew the outline of some waves with a pencil. She wanted to get the curls at the top just right. It was going to take a lot of paint to fill in the waves. Millie would do that at school.

Millie worked on the waves every afternoon
for the next two weeks, while the rest
of the class practised singing and dancing.
Isali finally learned all her dance moves,
and Millie had fun finishing the waves
for the set.

Chapter 4

Back on Stage

The night of the concert finally arrived. Millie skipped into the school hall, ready to show off her fabulous set design.

As soon as Dad and Millie walked in the school hall, Ms Perez rushed over. "Millie, Isali is unwell. She can't come tonight, so I need you to be the surfing seagull. You know all the dance moves."

Millie felt her stomach tighten.
She couldn't go on stage.
What if she fell over again?

"We really need you," said Jia.

Millie took a deep breath. "Okay,"
she said in a little voice.

Jia helped Millie to put on the seagull
costume. Millie's fingers were too shaky
to do up the buttons.

"Don't worry," said Jia. "You're a really
good dancer."

Millie stood on the stage and waited for
the music to start. She could hear her heart
beating in her ears. The music started
and her feet began to dance.

Suddenly, everyone was clapping.
It was over, and Millie was still on her feet!
She lined up with the other children and
proudly took a bow.

Millie couldn't stop smiling.
She remembered how much she loved
dancing. She was a set designer *and*
a performer!

Millie wasn't afraid of being on stage
any more. She couldn't wait for next
year's concert, and she thought about it
all the way home.